HENRY GASSER'S
GUIDE TO
PAINTING

PHOTOGRAPHS BY
FRANK PATTERSON

A GOLDEN HANDBOOK

GOLDEN PRESS
NEW YORK

FOREWORD

Since there are as many approaches to art as there are artists, the teaching of art becomes a very personal task. At the same time a book on the teaching of art takes on unusual responsibility because the person to person relationship is difficult to achieve in print.

Henry Gasser is no amateur at this difficult task. His seven books on painting, backed by his own competence, both as an artist and as a teacher, have made it possible for thousands of students to see art as Henry Gasser sees it. With this guidance the serious student can quickly move toward developing his own point of view, his own conceptions, and his own talents.

This book, which embodies the methods of Henry Gasser, is a stimulating and welcome addition to the Golden Handbook Series.

THE EDITORS

Other books by Henry Gasser
TECHNIQUES OF PICTURE MAKING
TECHNIQUES OF PAINTING THE WATERFRONT
TECHNIQUES OF PAINTING
OIL PAINTING METHODS AND DEMONSTRATIONS
CASEIN PAINTING METHODS AND DEMONSTRATIONS
HOW TO DRAW AND PAINT
WATERCOLOR—HOW TO DO IT

CONTENTS

INTRODUCTION

You can best learn to paint by painting—by experiencing for yourself the characteristics of every color on your palette, the qualities of each painting medium, the elusive problems of creating a subject on canvas or paper. But self-teaching is not enough; you must have instruction as well. This book is not meant to be a substitute for a good art school or a good teacher, but it can help you to learn the basic techniques of painting. It is a guide, *by example,* to painting with oil, watercolor and casein. It contains a multitude of illustrations and a minimum of text. This is how I paint; this is how most professional artists paint.

Depending on your level of study and talent, you can learn to use the same techniques by carefully following the demonstrations. Each demonstration develops a painting step by step. You can either re-create the identical painting or choose your own subject. I suggest the more original approach. This method is not only more challenging, but it will give you the freedom and pleasure of creating something of your own while you are learning. However, it would be a good idea to select subjects similar to mine. A summer landscape, for example, would obviously require different handling than a winter landscape.

Once you have grasped the fundamentals of all three painting mediums, you can select your favorite— the one which best fits your talent and temperament. Meanwhile, fill your sketch books!

H. G.

OIL PAINTING

I have chosen to open my book with the use of oil color because it is the most popular medium among students and professionals alike. It is also, perhaps, the easiest to work with. Don't be tempted, therefore, to do too much too soon. Begin with the discipline of a limited palette so that you will learn what can be accomplished with a single color before you try a second and a third. You should explore the nature of each color and its mixing properties before extending your range. Too frequently the beginner plunges into painting with a full palette, which is as unwise as starting to cook by putting every herb on the shelf into one dish. Once you have grasped the rudiments of mixing colors and handling the brush, you are ready to continue with the demonstrations. Each one adds some new element of technique, and gradually you will have the opportunity to do exercises in painting with the knife, underpainting, glazing and scumbling.

MATERIAL AND EQUIPMENT   I am assuming that the reader of this book has already acquired some of the material and equipment necessary for painting with oil color. Here is a quick check-up on your basic needs:

Charcoal Pencils or sticks for sketching on canvas.

Canvas—either stretched or on panels.

Brushes—at least six, including the following numbers: 2, 4, 6, 8, 10 (flats and brights).

Palette—either of wood or of metal. Also available is a disposable paper palette, which is becoming increasingly popular.

Oil Cup—that can be clipped to the palette. A double oil cup is preferable, one side reserved for turpentine, the other for the oil medium.

Palette Knife—for removing surplus or unwanted paint from the palette or canvas.

Fixative and Atomizer—for spraying a protective coating over the charcoal sketch to prevent smearing.

Colors—studio-size tubes are the most economical and are available in student and professional grades. See the following pages for list of colors.

Turpentine—needed for thinning of heavier oil mediums and general cleaning up.

Linseed Oil—for mixing with your colors.

Paint Box—or sketch box, as it is sometimes described, is necessary to hold all of the material above. A 12-by-16-inch size is most popular and is available in wood or metal.

Easel—the lid of the paint box can be used as an easel to hold canvas panels. This is feasible when painting outdoors and when you are using canvas panels up to 16-by-20 inches. I suggest obtaining a studio easel that will allow you to work in larger sizes; at the same time it provides a sturdy support.

Sketch Pad—an 8-by-10-inch (minimum size) sketch pad is necessary for planning compositions or drawing details for future reference.

As you progress you will gradually acquire more equipment, with brushes heading the list. Use brushes of good quality, and take care of them by cleaning them promptly and thoroughly after a painting session. Lukewarm water with soap is excellent; just make certain to remove all the soap through rinsing. Always reshape the brush by pressing the hairs with your thumb and forefinger while squeezing out the surplus water. (See page 12 for further information on brushes.)

You should explore painting mediums other than the conventional linseed oil and turpentine. Copal oil will give a bit more "pull" to your brush stroke. Sun-thickened and stand oils will do the same, and will impart a gloss to the surface of your painting.

In your initial attempts at oil painting you will find that panels made to the size of your paint box are the most convenient painting surface. These panels are generally made of an inexpensive cotton canvas glued over a stiff board. They may, on the other hand, be a composition board that has been pebbled to simulate canvas. As long as you are working fairly small and just gathering sketching material, the panels will suffice. However, at an early stage you should paint a subject on a stretched canvas. The resiliency of the surface is more receptive to your brush stroke and imparts more vitality to the painting. (See more about canvas on page 46.)

SELECTION AND MIXING OF COLORS   Twelve colors for a basic palette are shown on the facing page, reproduced at full intensity in the larger blocks. In the smaller blocks Zinc or Titanium White has been added. You can use this chart to establish the nature of a color. Frequently a color raw from the tube changes radically when it is mixed with white. Note how Viridian changes from a heavy, deep green to a delicate tint most useful when painting a sky. English Red, or Light Red, as it is popularly known, changes from a brownish red to a shade that is excellent for flesh tones. The same holds true of Yellow Ochre and Burnt Sienna—both important colors when painting a head. Raw Umber is a very useful color—not necessarily as a brown, but for the beautiful grays that can be produced when it is mixed with a blue. Mixed grays possess far more quality than a gray obtained by merely cutting black with white.

As you experiment with the mixing of color you will discover that some colors have a greater staining power than others. Thalo Blue is a typical example. It takes very little of this color to affect white paint, and it should be used with care.

Black is a difficult and sometimes dangerous color to use. Since it is a slow-drying color, it later may crack. It can be used sparingly to neutralize a color. Mars Black has been selected here because it has much faster drying qualities than Ivory or Lamp Black.

Alizarin Crimson is also a slow-drying color, but it is an important one, particularly for the landscape painter. Reduced with white it assumes a purplish tinge. If this effect is not desirable, use Alizarin Crimson Golden. It possesses a pleasing, warm quality when white is added. The remaining Cadmium colors

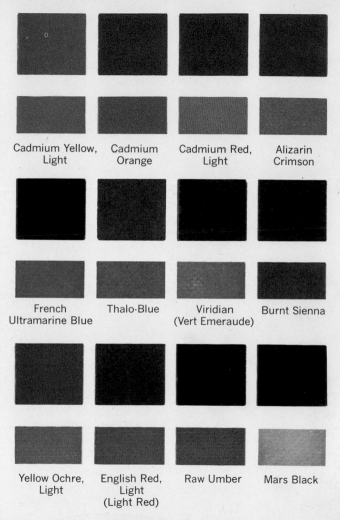

Cadmium Yellow, Light · Cadmium Orange · Cadmium Red, Light · Alizarin Crimson

French Ultramarine Blue · Thalo-Blue · Viridian (Vert Emeraude) · Burnt Sienna

Yellow Ochre, Light · English Red, Light (Light Red) · Raw Umber · Mars Black

courtesy M. Grumbacher, Inc.

and French Ultramarine Blue are excellent colors and can be mixed safely with the rest of the palette.

Additional Colors As you progress you will undoubtedly want to add more colors to your palette. On page 11 an additional dozen colors are suggested. Study the original color. See how it reacts when white is added. What I have said about the staining power of Thalo Blue applies also to Thalo Green and Thalo Yellow Green. Incidentally, the latter is one of the most vivid of the Thalo group, and it is almost impossible to achieve a similar color of its power by mixing yellow and blue. Another strong color is Indian Red. It differs from Light Red in that it becomes purplish when mixed.

Lemon Yellow and Cobalt Blue can frequently replace Cadmium Yellow Light and French Ultramarine Blue, particularly when a more delicate or softer color is desired. Burnt Umber and Cerulean Blue are fast-drying colors and, as such, are good for underpainting (p. 66). They also produce interesting grays when mixed together. Naples Yellow and Chromium Oxide Green—a beautiful grayed green—are two more colors that are excellent for underpainting. Payne's Gray is a bluish gray effective in neutralizing colors or in working with a restricted palette.

When you mix a color on your palette do not stir it too much or you may dull the mixture. Use of the palette knife for mixing will help you obtain a more vibrant color. When possible, try to mix the color directly on the canvas, particularly when you are working at a large size. Keep the use of white paint to a minimum. The white neutralizes your color and often causes a washed-out, chalky look.

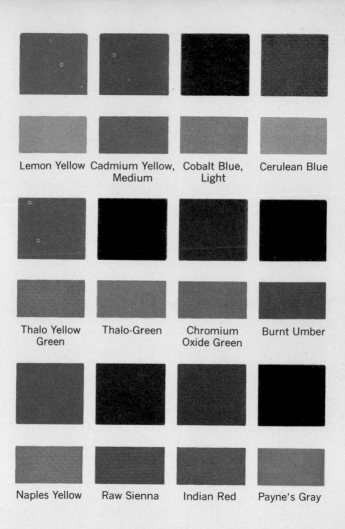

Lemon Yellow · Cadmium Yellow, Medium · Cobalt Blue, Light · Cerulean Blue

Thalo Yellow Green · Thalo-Green · Chromium Oxide Green · Burnt Umber

Naples Yellow · Raw Sienna · Indian Red · Payne's Gray

courtesy M. Grumbacher, Inc.

11

BRUSHES FOR OIL PAINTING The bulk of your painting will be done with bristle brushes. Use as large a brush as possible for the area you are covering. Frequently you can produce a thinner or finer stroke by using the brush edgewise.

Experiment with various strokes. By holding the brush loosely, near the end of the handle, a free, flowing line can be obtained; gripping the handle near the ferrule will produce a firmer stroke.

Shown below are five different types of brushes useful for oil painting. The first and most popular is the long-haired bristle brush. It produces a more fluid stroke than the short-haired bristle brush shown next. The short hairs impart vitality to a stroke, making this brush very useful for direct painting. The soft hair of the flat sable brush is very effective for a smooth finish and for blending. The round bristle brush is useful in obtaining various textural effects. Finally, there is the long-haired sable brush, which is very helpful in rendering fine lines and details.

Brushes courtesy M. Grumbacher, Inc.

BRUSH HANDLING

1 Most of the work is accomplished by holding the brush well away from the ferrule. This will provide better balance and permit a freer handling.

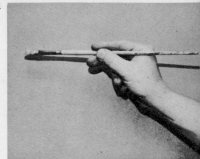

2 Grasp the brush by the ferrule for greater control when you want to depict a detail or use a sharp, vigorous stroke.

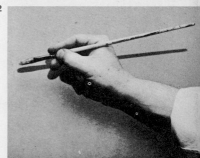

3 The brushwork can be varied by holding the brush in a club-like manner and rubbing or rolling the paint on the canvas.

LAY-IN OF THE SUBJECT The primary purpose of the lay-in is to establish the boundary lines of the composition. The lay-in can be indicated sketchily with the main lines of the composition, or it can be an elaborate, detailed monochromatic arrangement of light and dark. It is also possible to start out immediately with full color, dispensing with preliminary lines. However, this approach is for the professional and is generally used only for sketches.

Some instructors require their students to do a detailed composition before painting; other instructors ask only for a rough indication of the subject's principal elements. Both approaches have their advantages and disadvantages. An elaborate lay-in, for example, may tempt the student to adhere too rigidly to his composition, resulting in an unpleasantly tight painting. On the other hand, with only a rough sketch to guide him, the student can do a lot of fumbling and overpainting as he struggles to cover his canvas. If you feel that a detailed lay-in gives you more confidence for the subsequent painting, proceed accordingly. Or if a rough lay-in forces you to work harder in the painting of the subject, try that approach, for the struggle can often lend zest to your finished painting.

Consider these two factors in selecting your lay-in method: First, how complicated the subject is, and second, how well you can draw. Remove all trouble spots from a complex subject before you start to paint. Do this by making a variety of preliminary arrangements on paper (p. 36). If you are a good draughtsman you will see any structural weaknesses as the painting progresses and can correct them with a minimum amount of fumbling.

Six different approaches:
1 A rough charcoal drawing depicting the main lines of the subject. **2** A toned charcoal rendering. **3** A rough approach using oil paint. **4** Working directly with oil paint, toning the subject in a dry-brush manner. **5** Drawn with a fine brush and ink for detail. **6** The toning approach again, using medium (½ turpentine, ½ oil) to make the paint more fluid.

The subjects above are typical studies that can be painted with a single color and white. Experiment with different colors, learning their staining power and the range of values that can be achieved. At the same time these exercises will help to improve your brushwork.

KNOW YOUR COLORS Some teachers of art recommend that students work up elaborate color charts and color mixing exercises. These productions can be excellent devices for the studying of color, yet they can also be pitfalls. The student may assimilate various theories, but too frequently he puts only a small percentage of what he has learned into actual use. And there is the student who, although he produces wonderfully neat color charts, soon forgets their original purpose. Charts and color mixing exercises can still be helpful, however, particularly when working with transparent color. (Water-color, oil glazes, imprimatura, and so on.) I feel very strongly that the beginning artist will remember what a single color, or a combination of colors, can do if it is related to depicting a subject.

On the facing page are shown three monochromatic illustrations. Such studies serve several purposes. You learn the range of a particular color; you discover that the darker the color the greater the range; and you determine the staining power of a color. For example, the color chart does not show too great a difference when Viridian Green is placed beside Thalo Green, as both are used at full strength. However, by mixing a dab of each of the greens with white paint, the greater saturation power of Thalo Green is immediately evident. As you do these monochromatic studies, you will also discover how some colors change considerably when mixed with white, while other colors retain their identity. Finally, these studies can provide helpful exercises in the handling of your brushes (p. 33). Without varying color to divert the eye, the brushwork becomes much more apparent.

USING TWO COLORS   It is natural for the novice to believe that the more colors he has on his palette at the start the greater a variety of colors he will be able to mix. It is not until the novice becomes more experienced that he begins to discern the weakness of using too many colors. Every color you add to your palette increases the chances of producing a discordant note; the fewer colors you employ the better are your chances of obtaining a harmonious effect. By limiting your palette at the outset, you are forced to discover the full possibilities of each color as you work.

On the facing page are three examples of results obtained by using a warm and a cool color. The illustration at the top combines Cerulean Blue with Yellow Ochre. (It is understood that White paint is also included whenever using oil color.) As neither of these colors possesses a great range from light to dark, the interpretation of the subject is limited to a medium to high key. The center sketch demonstrates the effect of combining Thalo Blue and Raw Umber. Both of these colors have a wider range from light to dark than the colors used previously, as the illustration reveals. In the final example, the subject has been painted with Cobalt Blue and Burnt Sienna. Both of these colors possess a pleasing range and seem to have an affinity for each other.

I suggest that you go through some of your old sketches or paintings, selecting those that you think could be simplified and rendered with two colors. Use the colors that have been mentioned, and also make up your own combinations. When you do the latter, prepare a graded blending of the two colors before attempting to paint the subject. The blending will provide you with a preview of the color range you can achieve.

The illustration at the top combines Cerulean Blue with Yellow Ochre. The center sketch combines Thalo Blue and Raw Umber. In the final example, the subject has been painted with Cobalt Blue and Burnt Sienna.

USING THREE COLORS We are now ready to add a third color to our palette. A warm yellow and red are used with Cobalt Blue. These approximate the three primary colors, so we can readily establish a wide range of additional colors. Also, subtle grays can be produced to enhance brightly painted areas.

Cadmium Yellow, Med.

Cadmium Red, Lt.

Cobalt Blue

OIL DEMONSTRATION 1:
Using Three Colors

1 Establish the lay-in with Cobalt Blue, using the dry-brush technique shown on page 15 (fig. 4). Now paint the sky, using yellow generously cut with white. Add a bit of blue at the zenith. Then, again in a dry-brush manner, rough in some of the foreground colors.

2 Add more color to the foreground, especially the warm tones. Then paint

1

2

the background. Once all the essential colors have been indicated, paint them in a more solid manner.

3 Apply final color to the foreground, somewhat thinly in the shadow areas and more heavily in the light. Paint the grass and rock textures, as well as some ripples in the water area.

3

VARYING THREE COLORS You will note that the yellow and blue mixtures do not vary much from the colors previously used. However, Alizarin Crimson is quite different from Cadmium Red Light. Because it is a cool red, when mixed with blue it can create a vibrant violet, while Cadmium Red Light (a warm red) results in a deadened purplish mixture.

Cadmium
Yellow, Lt.

Alizarin
Crimson

French
Ultramarine

OIL DEMONSTRATION 2:
Varying Three Colors

1 After doing a lay-in (use French Ultramarine), paint the sky of the subject in a loose style roughly suggesting the cloud formation. Note the grays used in the clouds. Next paint the deep green trees against the sky, and indicate a bit of ground.

2 Now paint in the rocks, still applying the color loosely. Then paint the background, keeping the color

1

grayed slightly to make it recede. Next paint the water area, roughly portraying its motion.

3 Add the brighter colors, and the subject will come into focus. Refine the entire canvas. Finally, define the cloud formation, and render details in the rock and water areas.

GRAYED PRIMARY COLORS   In this exercise we use *grayed* primary colors. The regular yellow is changed to Yellow Ochre; the red, to Light Red—more of an earth color; and the blue, to Payne's Gray. I believe this demonstration is of the utmost importance, for it introduces the use of muted color harmony.

Yellow Ochre

Light Red

Payne's Gray

OIL DEMONSTRATION 3:

Grayed Primary Colors

1   After doing a lay-in with Payne's Gray, spot areas with Yellow Ochre and Light Red. Working in a direct manner, lightly paint the local colors in the foreground, allowing some of the canvas to show through.

2   With the foreground and the background partially covered, paint in the sky, and

1

2

emphasize the cloud shapes to impart a dramatic effect. At the same time, solidly paint the distant houses to silhouette them sharply.

3 If you now have too cool an effect, introduce warm color into the sky area. Gradually paint the canvas in more solid fashion, adding warmer tones. Place details and sharp accents wherever necessary.

3

SKETCHING ON THE SPOT The term "sketching" is generally thought to mean a black and white impression of a subject. Actually, a sketch can be rendered in any medium.

The sketches shown on the facing page illustrate the same subject in three different mediums. First, we have the black and white sketch treated with a felt-tipped pen. This is the quickest and most convenient way to capture an impression of the subject, using a minimum amount of equipment. Tonal values can be obtained, but color is sacrificed. However, penciled notations, depicting the colors observed, can provide a guide for developing a painting later in the studio (pp. 134–136). This method can be applied successfully only after a long period of painting on the spot, learning directly from nature.

The second illustration is an oil version of the same subject. Oil painting is undoubtedly the best medium for grasping and reworking the subject in a direct, straightforward manner. Changes in drawing, values and color can be made quickly and with relative ease.

The third illustration interprets the subject with watercolor. This medium is best expressed in a direct manner, and it is more difficult to handle than oil. But once the technique is mastered, it is excellent for capturing fleeting effects.

I suggest that you try working outdoors in various mediums until you find the one suitable to your temperament and talent. As you progress you will also discover that certain subjects lend themselves more readily to oil, others to watercolor. Later you may wish to create a studio painting from an outdoor sketch; you can then switch to your favorite indoor medium.

A felt pen sketch.

An oil sketch.

A watercolor sketch.

SKETCHING IN BLACK AND WHITE   I am constantly experimenting with sketching mediums, but my favorite, in the black and white, is the felt pen. Although it has been designed primarily for broad, bold effects, through special handling a variety of effects can be achieved. The drawings shown above provide a few examples. They vary from simple blacks combined with dry-brush strokes to a heavy, fluid handling, and finally, to a delicate, semi-dry technique.

I suggest that you carry two felt pens on your sketching trip. In one, have the ink running fluid for use in the large black areas. Keep the second pen on the dry side, restricting its use to the light or gray areas.

Experiment on different types of paper. Rough, absorbent paper may impart an interesting dry-brush texture. Smooth paper may allow the felt tip to glide quickly over its surface, capturing a fleeting effect.

Various colored inks are available for the felt tip pen, but I find that most of them are too vivid. The one exception is brown; you may want to use this color as a change of pace from the usual black.

Along with the making of sketches you will want to accumulate studies. These studies can be prepared for the subject you are presently working on or for future use. If your painting includes a bit of complicated architecture, it will be wise to make a few detailed studies of that area. You may only suggest it in the final painting, but the study will help you decide what to omit.

Certain subjects lend themselves to studies—trees, for example. Their anatomy can be observed in the winter months, their foliage in the summer. People at work and play—their postures and walk, their gestures—are also subjects that can be incorporated into future paintings.

Much of the material you will accumulate may play only a small part in the masterpiece you are painting. But that part will be done convincingly when a disciplined study of nature has been the source.

THE SKETCH BOOK   Along with its use in planning compositional sketches for a painting, the sketch book can serve several purposes. When time is limited, you can make thumbnail sketches or fragmentary notes. When time is not important, but you do not have your painting equipment on hand, elaborate drawings can be made and, as I said earlier, supplemented with penciled notations indicating the color. And then there is the sketch that is made just for the pure enjoyment of sketching!

Experiment with mediums other than pencil. Try pen and ink—excellent for a more disciplined approach. For a completely different approach, use a piece of conté crayon and apply it in a broad manner. The felt-tipped pen, with its interchangeable nibs, also offers interesting possibilities.

FINDING SUBJECTS TO SKETCH The sketches on this page were all made in the same block. This happens to be one of the many intriguing streets in Rockport, Massachusetts. Carrying a small 8-by-10-inch sketch pad and a felt-tipped pen, I strolled along, stopping to make a sketch of whatever arrangement struck my fancy. While it is true that this particular area is very picturesque, there are a lot of "Rockports" to be found throughout the country if you look for them. The subject matter may range from metropolitan street scenes to industrial plants, but it is all worth recording through the painter's eye.

SKETCHING MATERIAL AND EQUIPMENT When working outdoors you will want to travel as lightly as possible. Sketching in black and white is a simple matter, for little material is needed. Oil or watercolor is more of a problem. Tubes of color, brushes, canvas panels, watercolor paper, and so forth, can bulk up and become unwieldy.

There is a portable combination easel and paint box available which simplifies the carrying of equipment. It folds up to compact size and is conveniently held. When opened (see illustration) it becomes a sturdy easel with plenty of working space and easy access to paints and brushes. While designed primarily for oil painters, it can be quickly converted to a carrier of watercolor or casein equipment. If you prefer to work in a seated position, the only extra equipment you will need is a folding sketching stool.

When planning a sketching trip, always check on your supplies. I cannot think of anything more frustrating than to run short on white paint miles from your studio or find that you have omitted your favorite color! Include plenty of paint rags, and don't forget your sketch book for preliminary compositional notations and details.

When working outdoors you will find it easier to capture subjects quickly and convincingly if you paint with the form—that is, employing brush strokes which follow the contours of the subject. The above sketches show how brushwork can follow the various forms found in nature.

A Color Study

STUDIES AND SKETCHES   Painting on the spot generally falls into two categories—the study and the sketch. The latter is a spontaneous interpretation or impression of the subject and is complete in itself. A study is a probing observation of the subject—a single detail or a series of details, perhaps later to be incorporated into a studio painting.

The painting above is a cloud formation study. The strip of land at the base was included only to help establish a value note against the sky. I was interested in searching for—and then painting—the soft and hard edges of the clouds. At the same time I was relating the formation to the background of blue sky,

34

A Color Sketch

noting how the latter lightened as it approached the horizon. A study such as this serves two purposes. First, it reveals a little more knowledge about the anatomy of a cloud and the nature of surrounding atmospheric effects. Second, it can be used as a reference for a studio painting in which a similar sky appears.

You will find that your studies and sketches, whether in color or black and white, comprehensive or fragmentary, will prove invaluable for future work. Only after several years thus observing directly from nature will you be able to produce studio painting with authority.

Preliminary compositional sketches do not have to be carefully drawn. They should be of an exploratory nature—a search for the best possible composition of the scene before you. The light and dark areas should be depicted, however roughly, as an aid in determining the entire pattern or design of the subject.

PAINTING OUTDOORS In starting to paint outdoors we rely on the old standby—a red barn against a summer background. No matter how familiar the subject may be, it is how we interpret it that will keep it from being commonplace. A basic safeguard is to compose it into as strong a design as possible.

Carry a small sketch book on all of your sketching trips for making preliminary compositions. At the left is a page from my sketch book. Using the barn grouping as the center of interest, I did several quick arrangements. While they varied in size, all of them scaled roughly to a 12-by-16-inch proportion. This was the size of the canvas panel in my sketch box. After I had decided on the arrangement that I thought would be the most interesting, I sketched it on the panel, as shown below, using charcoal as my medium.

1

2

OIL DEMONSTRATION 4: An Outdoor Subject

1 Do a charcoal sketch, as on page 37.

2 Quickly make a blue lay-in over the charcoal sketch. Using the paint in a fluid manner, roughly indicate the shaded areas. At the same time, loosely establish a tonal range, varying the blue according to the depth of the shadows.

3 Before the blue lay-in is dry, start to spot colors in the dark areas, roughly. Concentrate only on the color, without too much concern

about forms. Apply the paint loosely, allowing the canvas and lay-in to show through partially in spots.

4 Continue to paint the subject as in the previous stage, gradually working from the dark color areas to the light. The entire canvas will be coarsely covered with paint, and you should make an overall check of the color values. Now you can start refining the color and shapes of the various objects and smoothing out the roughly painted areas. At this point,

3

you may want to change from stiff bristle brushes to a soft-haired, flat sable brush. Finally, put in enough detail to suggest texture and to sharpen the overall finish.

4

OIL DEMONSTRATION 5: A Summer Subject

1   Cut Yellow Ochre with a fast-drying medium, and cover the canvas. Then, use the same color to brush in the composition.

2   As colors (Alizarin Crimson, Raw Umber, Viridian, Thalo Blue and Cadmium Orange) are applied over the wet Yellow Ochre, they pick

up some of its tone, to create a warm, pleasing effect.

3 At the horizon add Cobalt Blue to the water, and blend light Yellow Ochre into the blue of the sky. Mix Cadmium Yellow Light with the blues for the greens of distant hills.

4 Add Cadmium Red Light to the Alizarin Crimson to brighten up the barrel and part of the boat house. Render rigging on boats, and indicate seagulls.

OIL DEMONSTRATION 6: A Winter Subject

1 In doing a winter subject you may also give the canvas a preliminary toning. Mix a cool, neutral color. Cover the canvas, and then brush in the main lines of the composition.

2 First roughly paint in the dark trees and shaded areas of the houses, and then the white in part of the snow. The neutral toning forms a halftone, allowing you to establish light and dark notes.

3

3 Now lay in the background. Normally the sky area would be painted next. However, if the original toning looks pleasing in color and value, as it does in the illustration, allow it to serve as the sky. Paint the dark leaves of the trees.

4 Now paint the rest of the snow area, and with this, all the colors needed to depict the subject have been applied. To complete the painting add more solid paint in the light area, refine passages of color and, finally, put in the sharp details.

4

REWORKING A PAINTING   As you work outdoors you will find yourself building up a collection of paintings that have served their purpose by helping you to record scenes directly from nature. As sketches or studies they are complete in themselves. However, you have undoubtedly painted some subjects that did not quite come up to your expectations. Possibly you did not have enough time to finish them, or perhaps the color values were unsatisfactory in certain areas.

The painting reproduced above is such an example. It had turned out rather flat, and I thought of experimenting to see if it could be brightened up. First I darkened and at the same time strengthened the

modeling of the trees. This immediately gave the painting a lift. It was then necessary to eliminate the hard edge of the trees where they met the sky, so I repainted the sky. This helped to obtain soft edges in the tree area. At the same time I introduced some clouds to break the monotony of the sky. The next step was to brighten the barn by repainting it a more vivid red. By now the subject had perked up considerably, but the foreground was still too dull. Strokes of pure color blended into the existing color keyed it with the rest of the painting. Some details were then sharply delineated.

The reworked painting is shown above.

45

STUDIO PAINTING   After a period of painting and sketching directly from nature, you should attempt to develop a studio painting selected from the material you have accumulated. The studio painting serves several purposes:

Assuming you have acquired enough background in painting outdoors, it allows you to develop a more vital and possibly a more creative interpretation of the subject. There are no size limitations (although this does not mean the bigger the painting the better the result). You do not have to be concerned with changing light, weather, inquisitive bystanders, and so forth. You can work at whatever pace you want to set and, generally, stop painting at any stage. You can take more time to think about the painting, and if you encounter a problem, pause to make a separate sketch. You can take time to prepare the canvas, applying special surfaces to achieve interesting textures for overpainting, and special color grounds that enhance the color applied over them (pp. 66–73).

Equipment in the Studio   We would all prefer to have a large studio with a north lighted skylight, but unfortunately most of us have to compromise. Actually, just a bit of improvisation will make any room suitable. Only in portrait painting is it imperative for you and the sitter to have an even, steady light.

There is one piece of equipment that is an absolute necessity whatever the lighting conditions—a substantial easel. The outdoor easel recommended on page 32 is excellent when used indoors for small canvases, but for large paintings you need a studio easel. A big help: a high stool for sitting in front of the canvas when you tire of standing. Also, unless you are painting a portrait, have an additional stool or table on which to rest your palette.

I find it convenient to have on hand several sizes of stretched blank canvases. I also have ready a few canvases with a toning of gray or tan. With these a harmonious effect can be more quickly achieved than by painting into a dead white surface.

The canvas you choose can vary in texture according to the effect you are attempting to convey. Generally, a heavy, rough-textured canvas is most suitable for landscape. On the other hand, a smooth canvas is more appropriate for a portrait or highly detailed still life.

Canvas is available in cotton and linen. The former is less expensive but, being more absorbent, has a tendency to draw the color from the painting. Linen is more permanent; use it whenever possible.

When working from day to day on a studio painting, you may want to apply retouch varnish to brighten up areas where the paint appears dull. If the area is dry to the touch, apply the varnish with a soft brush; if still tacky, use a spray. Special pressure cans of retouch varnish are available. They are convenient and inexpensive.

As the painting progresses you will undoubtedly reach a troublesome section. Rather than keep repainting, you might consider using your palette knife. Scrape down to the bare canvas, or at least remove the excess paint. You will have a much better surface on which to work. Too frequently the student, in attempting to repaint a faulty area, succeeds only in building up unpleasant layers of paint.

OIL DEMONSTRATION 7: A Studio Summer Subject

1 Make a fairly comprehensive charcoal rendering,
and spray with fixatif. Then
thinly apply either French
Ultramarine or Cobalt Blue.
You will now have a pattern of
light and dark.

2 Now, using full color
(Light Red, Cobalt Blue,
Alizarin Crimson, Yellow
Ochre and Viridian), start
painting thinly again in the
large areas. Attempt to arrive
at only the approximate

color. Where necessary, add a small amount of White to lighten color.

3 Paint the background and sky. Then build up the light areas. You may want to switch from bristle brushes to a soft-haired brush when painting over a wet area.

4 Now paint the details. A "rigger" or pointed brush might be easier to use for boat rigging, lettering, and the like. Check the overall effect. Sharpen or soften edges; blend or subdue the color. Finally, place sharp accents.

TRANSFERRING A SKETCH   When you have selected the sketch you want to develop into a large painting, there are several ways to enlarge it to the desired size. The most common approach is illustrated on the facing page and is known as the "squaring up" method. As you see, the sketch has been squared and the canvas, shown below, has been squared in correspondingly larger areas. This method has the advantage of enabling one to obtain an enlargement speedily and accurately. Its disadvantage is that when the original sketch is not too well composed its weaknesses are magnified on the large canvas.

Any problems or weaknesses in composition should therefore be resolved at the sketch stage since they become more difficult to resolve in the larger size. At the sketch stage you tend to deal with the subject with greater spontaneity, a quality you should try to retain in your studio paintings.

There are many artists who shun any enlarging device and believe that the sketch should be transferred free hand to the canvas. Then you can shorten, elongate, add or eliminate any areas that will help strengthen the composition. I myself somewhat prefer this approach, particularly when I have concentrated more on color than on arrangement in my original sketch.

I suggest that you let the nature of the original sketch determine the method you use. If the original sketch possesses a lot of detail in certain areas, it may be feasible to square up only those sections. Or, you may want to transfer only the main lines of the original composition and gradually develop the details free hand.

A WINTER SUBJECT IN OIL   The difficulties encoun-
tered with weather make it more practical to paint
winter subjects in the comfort of the studio.

In setting the mood of the winter subject, however,
and in expressing subtle snow effects, your powers of
observation and the accuracy of your on-the-spot
sketches will be put to their greatest test. The extra
time you spend in making such notes will prove invaluable for painting indoors. To paint a snow scene of any
distinction you will find that obvious blues and purples
must be toned down.

OIL DEMONSTRATION 8: A Studio Winter Subject

1 Essentially, the painting of a winter subject in the
studio is accomplished with
the same approach used in

2

3

53

the previous demonstration. First do a charcoal drawing of the subject. Still using charcoal, roughly indicate the arrangement of light and shadow. When this is rendered, spray the charcoal with fixatif.

2 (See page 53.) Paint the dark areas first, applying the color in a loose manner. Be careful to make the tones deep enough, for it is easier to lighten these areas later

than it is to darken them.

3 (See page 53.) Work over entire canvas, applying the color loosely. Remember to keep the paint fairly thin, scraping it down wherever it accumulates too heavily.

4 Illustration 4 shows how the painting should look at this stage, with details only crudely indicated. If you are doubtful about the color or shape of an area, changes

5

should be made at this stage. This is important; it will keep you from overpainting areas in the final stage, which often produces an unpleasant surface quality in a painting.

5   Before going on to the final stage as shown here, it may be advisable to use retouch varnish. The varnish will bring out the color of any areas that may have dried dull and, at the same time, produce a better working surface. Spray the varnish on the painting instead of using a brush, to prevent smearing. Then complete the painting.

Note: The colors used for this demonstration are Thalo Blue, Yellow Ochre, Alizarin Crimson, Raw Umber, Cobalt Blue, Viridian, Light Red, Cadmium Red Light and a touch of Mars Black.

PALETTE KNIFE PAINTING   A palette knife was recommended earlier for keeping the palette clean, scraping, and the occasional mixing of colors. However, a *painting* knife is used in applying color to the canvas. This instrument is far more flexible than the palette knife and is available in a number of shapes and sizes. Two popular painting knives are shown below.

You can combine knife painting with your regular brush painting to achieve interesting effects. For example, a strong highlight can be achieved far more effectively, and faster, by using the painting knife. Color passages that have become dull through continual brushing can be given a bright, new vitality when fresh color is applied over the deadened passages with this knife. And it can be used as a painting implement complete in itself.

On the facing page is a group of sketches that have been made solely with a painting knife. It is an excellent method of achieving sparkling color effects and, at the same time, avoiding tightness.

A trowel-shaped, short blade gives a more vigorous stroke in contrast to the longer blade. The latter is useful when a more delicate (sensitive) handling of the point is desired.

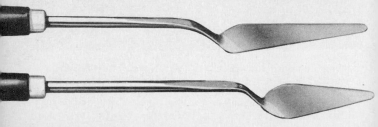

While the term "palette-knife sketches" is used to describe the examples above, they are actually done with a painting knife. In this series the subject was sketched roughly in charcoal and then dusted lightly. A faint image remained to guide the application of color.

1

OIL DEMONSTRATION 9: Using the Palette Knife

1 Make a charcoal sketch, and dust off lightly, leaving a faint image. Then, using a painting knife, apply the color. Try to get the color as true as possible from the start.

2 Spot the color so that you can quickly relate one area

2

3

to another. Concentrate on the color. You can always recapture the drawing.

3 Continue the painting, still relating adjacent areas. Frequently you can mix a color directly on the canvas, especially in large areas.

4 When the canvas is completely covered, check the color values and refine the various passages.

4

STILL-LIFE PAINTING   In his early years of study the student is primarily concerned with learning how to draw. His models may vary from a still life composed of a couple of books, to a head posed by a sympathetic friend. In any event, he eliminates the problem of color by simply ignoring it and generally concentrating on a penciled outline followed by shading with the same pencil. In his early childhood he "expressed" himself with colored crayons or with non-toxic paints. But only his teacher and a few other adults were able to discern what "message" his choice of colors was conveying. He remained happily ignorant! Then there was the school in which color was the dessert served only after some years of drawing restricted to black and white.

Fortunately, the artist who becomes interested in landscape will be vitally concerned with color. And for the rest of his days he will constantly be seeking new color effects and new color schemes.

One of the best ways to develop an eye for color, values, drawing, and handling of paint is by painting still lifes. It may not be your ambition to become famous as a painter of such subjects, but that is beside the point. Still-life painting allows you, in the quiet of your studio, to study without interruption the objects before you—their most subtle nuances of color, the color effects of various textures, the nature of color reflections, and the like. It is, in other words, an opportunity to explore many painting problems. You can control the color scheme from the start by selecting the objects to be painted. At the same time you can plan a varying textural arrangement, such as a pebble-textured orange beside the semi-sheen of an apple, both placed on a shining white plate, or a rough drapery seen against the polish of a glass vase. This concentrated study of textures will help you not only in still-life painting but will prove invaluable later when applied to the painting of landscapes.

An important point to remember in doing a still life is to plan as interesting and as exciting an arrangement as possible at the start, thereby sustaining your interest throughout the painting.

OIL DEMONSTRATION 10: A Still Life

1 Take time to arrange the still life so that the color and shape of the various objects complement each other

1

Make several arrangements until you arrive at the one that seems to be the most interesting. Then make only a rough charcoal sketch of the subject; most of the color work is to be done with the knife. Start spotting the various colors, making no attempt to cover the entire area of each object. Concentrate on the relationship of each color to the one adjacent. Reminder: wipe the knife with a paint rag every so often.

2 Continue working until all of the objects are roughly colored on the canvas. The original surface should show through in the lightest areas. Paint the background in the same manner, still retaining portions of the original canvas. Have the strokes of your knife follow the form of the various objects where you

2

feel it will strengthen their shape. At the conclusion of this stage you should have a rudimentary color arrangement. Make any changes necessary at this point.

3 Now paint the light areas, gradually covering the original white canvas that has been retained until this stage. As the canvas disappears the objects will take shape, and the resulting surface will be one of varying thickness of paint—typical when color is applied with a knife. If the paint is too heavy in some areas, remove it with the edge of your knife. Again, you may want to smooth a surface—such as the tablecloth; this can be done by keeping the knife as flat as possible. To finish the painting, put in sharp accents, applying paint with the tip of the knife.

3

USING A COLOR BASE Another approach to palette-knife painting is to first stain the canvas with the approximate colors of the subject. This is particularly effective when your time is limited or when you wish to capture a fleeting mood.

The main lines of the subject are quickly sketched with charcoal. Then, with a piece of rag or a soft brush dipped in turpentine, color is applied. No attempt is made to delineate the various forms. Instead, with the oil paint reduced to an almost watery consistency, the basic elements of the subject are depicted.

Later, in the studio, the subject can be developed by applying paint over the stained areas with a palette knife.

OIL DEMONSTRATION 11: Using a Color Base

1 Prepare an on-the-spot sketch in color, using only enough color to guide you later in the palette-knife painting.

2 With the color-stained canvas serving as a base, repaint the subject, using the palette knife. Wherever possible, make your strokes fol-

low the form of the object being painted. The reproduction above shows the color-stained canvas almost completely repainted.

3 Now modify some of the raw color that was applied in the previous stage. Intensify the color in other areas, repainting the highlights in a much heavier manner and flattening the darks somewhat for contrast. Add accents wherever you find them necessary. When these touches are in place, the painting is completed.

UNDERPAINTING AND GLAZING Underpainting is a method that enables you to obtain textural surfaces that are virtually impossible to accomplish through direct painting. A simple approach to underpainting is shown on this and the facing page. Below are three examples showing the preliminary work needed before using color. The first subject was painted with a knife, in a quick-drying white, in this instance MG White for underpainting. The contours of the rocks were strongly modeled with the form, allowing the ridges resulting from the knife to remain. When dry—it generally takes from two to four hours—a warm color glaze was applied over the light areas. This was followed by cool glazes applied over the shadowed areas. The result is shown on the opposite page.

A glaze is obtained by cutting your oil paint to a watery consistency, producing a stain of the original color, and mixing it with one part copal varnish to five parts turpentine. This is then mixed with your regular oil color to whatever staining strength you wish. There is also a commercial medium known as Gel that is handier to use. Clear and color-less and of a vaseline-like quality, it reduces the con-sistency of oil paint to a transparent color without making it fluid. Whether you are using Gel or a medium which you have mixed yourself to pro-duce a glaze, always be certain to apply it with a soft brush.

The second example shows the underpainted white applied with a stiff brush in a pouncing-like motion. A similar texture can be obtained by using a sponge instead of the brush. Glazing and some direct painting followed the underpainting, with the results shown.

The final subject, de-picting a cluster of trees, was painted with short strokes by knife and then glazed when dry.

Underpainting does not have to be white. It can be done with modi-fied or grayed colors and then brought up to full color through a series of successive glazes.

French Ultramarine
Glaze over Cadmium
Red, Light

Alizarin Crimson
Glaze over Cadmium
Yellow, Medium

Burnt Sienna Glaze
over Oxide of
Chromium Green

Viridian Glaze
over Naples Yellow
mixed with White

Thalo Blue Glaze
over Cadmium Red,
Light mixed with
White

Light Red Glaze over
Cadmium Yellow,
Light mixed with White

Shown here are a few exercises that illustrate how
the staining power of glazes varies in affecting an
undercolor that was allowed to dry. In each case the

pure glaze is shown at the top of the oblong. The center section illustrates its effect over the undercolor. The undercolor alone is shown at the bottom.

You will discover that some colors such as Alizarin Crimson, Viridian, Rose Madder, Burnt Sienna, Green Earth and the Ultramarines possess a transparent quality in their original state. Frequently they can be used for glazing just as they come from the tube, adding your regular medium to make them workable. Look through some of your past paintings (oil or watercolor) and select a subject which, although fairly simple, contains enough material to present various textures. The painting shown below is a good example of what I mean. The wood-framed house against the soft foliage, the warm dirt road, the stone wall and steps—all aid in creating interesting texture and color.

In this demonstration I preferred to work on a rigid surface, a linen canvas panel, because I planned to build a fairly heavy underpainting. Using my original painting as a guide, I redrew the subject in charcoal, then dusted the charcoal lightly, leaving a faint image.

After you have chosen a suitable painting, proceed step-by-step, as in the demonstration.

The spot sketch used as a guide.

69

OIL DEMONSTRATION 12: Underpainting and Glazing

1 After you have sketched in the subject with charcoal spray it with fixatif. Then apply a single color toning over the canvas. Here Cobalt Blue was used, cut to a thin consistency with copal oil painting medium. At the conclusion of this step the visual effect should be the same as the monochromatic lay-in of previously painted demon-

1

strations. It will dry in a short time, and you will be able to resume with the next step.

2 Now paint with white the light areas and those requiring special textural effects. In this demonstration I used MG White for underpainting. Apply the paint with both brush and knife, depending on the texture you desire. At this point you can resort to any implement that will help to create unusual effects, such as a stencil brush, sponge, cheesecloth, and so on. The painting should be allowed to dry thoroughly before you take the next step.

3 The surface of the painting is now ready for you to add color glazes. You must, of course, choose these to suit your subject. Here, I applied a warm yellow glaze over the entire canvas, rubbing it with a clean rag where I did not want it to appear too strong. Where a warmer glaze was required, such as the sunlit areas of the road, roof and tree trunks, Cadmium Orange was added to the yellow glaze. Over the shaded area of the stone wall and steps I applied a grayish-tone glaze.

3

4 When the glazed areas are dry to the touch, paint in a more direct manner. Referring to your original painting for color and detail, cover the various areas gradually, applying the color thinly to display the full texture of the underpainting in certain areas or painting in a heavier manner to subdue the texture. When the painting is completed it will be glossier in some of the glazed areas than in others. A coating of retouch varnish will quickly give an even sheen to the entire surface.

SCUMBLING   In contrast to glazing, which intensifies the underlying color, scumbling is generally used to lighten a previously painted area. That area must be dry and the paint applied over it in a dragging motion, producing a broken effect of color. Mix the required colors just as the paint comes from the tubes and apply with a bristle brush. Semi-opaque colors such as Yellow Ochre, Lemon Yellow and Permanent Green Light, or opaque colors such as Cerulean Blue, Naples Yellow, the Umbers, Chromium Oxide Green, Red Earth and Mars colors, are all useful for scumbling.

When employing this technique you will frequently find that a pleasing effect can be obtained by allowing some of the original undercolor to show through. Interesting textures, the softening or subduing of strong, raw color, the obliteration of unnecessary details, all can be accomplished through scumbling.

As you experiment, you may want to work with semi-transparent color. Often a dull passage of dark color can be relieved or unified just by producing a lighter veil of color over it. A small amount of your regular painting medium can be mixed with the color to help make it semi-transparent. At the same time a softer brush will help to apply the color in a smooth, even manner. The consistency of the paint and different methods of application will produce great variety in the quality of scumbling. Be sure to remember that the area of canvas to be scumbled should always be dry. This makes possible the broken color which creates the most exciting textural effects.

I suggest you take some of your old paintings and use them for experimenting with various scumbling methods. You may even be able to salvage them for a future exhibition!

WATERCOLOR

Watercolor is a somewhat more difficult medium than oil in its demands for greater facility in brush handling and greater deftness. Consequently I have taken more space in the watercolor section than in Oil Painting to illustrate brushwork. You will learn eventually that watercolor has its devices—tricks, as some people call them—to achieve effects not possible with oil. Before you experiment with these devices, however, I will guide you through color exercises similar to those done with oil. Again, your palette should be limited at the start. By the time you come to the use of a full palette and have the special devices at your command as well, you will see why watercolor is worth the trouble.

MATERIAL AND EQUIPMENT   Watercolor paints and material are available in professional and student grades. In your early attempts, good results can be obtained with the less expensive student-grade items with one possible exception—and that is watercolor paper. In no other medium is the working surface so vital for successful results. The best paper is hand-made of 100 percent linen rag cotton and is available in different weights. A 140-lb. weight is heavy enough for most work, with 70 lbs. the minimum weight for small painting. If you do use a student-grade or machine-made paper, select as heavy a weight as possible.

The usual sheet of watercolor paper (Imperial size) is 22 by 30 inches. It can be cut in half or quartered to smaller working sizes. The quarter size (11 by 15 inches) makes a nice workable size for outdoor spot sketches. You may prefer to work on a watercolor block. A block consists of a number of sheets glued together around the edges. It is convenient to carry and is available in several different sizes. I advise you to obtain a block of fairly heavy paper, for paper lighter in weight will buckle when moistened.

Watercolor paper is made with various surface finishes. The rough finish (R) and the cold pressed finish (C.P.) are the most popular. A very smooth finish, not too frequently used by watercolorists, is the hot pressed paper (H.P.). I personally prefer the cold pressed finish because it provides enough texture to make an interesting and receptive painting surface. The rough finish is excellent for large studio paintings and will take considerable handling, texturing and washing out of unwanted color passages.

You can also obtain watercolor paper, with the finishes mentioned, mounted on cardboard. The rigid backing is most helpful when doing a detailed or architectural subject.

Selection and Mixing of Colors If you use the best watercolor paper, I believe you can obtain good results at the start with student-grade colors. As you paint and progress, I am certain you will gradually switch to the best grade of professional colors. These colors have better saturating power and permanency.

In choosing colors, you will find that many of those on your oil color list are available in watercolor. The following permanent colors are recommended for your basic palette:

Alizarin Crimson, Cadmium Red Light, Cadmium

Yellow Light, Cadmium Orange, Light Red, Yellow Ochre, Burnt Sienna, French Ultramarine, Ivory Black, Viridian, Thalo Blue.

You might wish to add the following colors to supplement the above list. They will also be useful in doing the watercolor exercises recommended later in this section:

Cobalt Blue, Raw Sienna, Hookers Green, Thalo Green, Alizarin Crimson (Golden), Chromium Oxide Green, Payne's Gray, Burnt Umber, Davy's Gray, Cerulean Blue

Earlier in the book I said that color mixing charts were not too important. However, in working with transparent watercolor (in contrast to opaque oil paint) such charts can help you to acquire technical control —and in watercolor this is very important—and also to learn the particular qualities of your colors. While all watercolors are basically transparent, they vary in the *degree* of transparency. Heavier pigments tend to the opaque. Yellow Ochre, Cerulean Blue, Chromium Oxide Green are typical examples. Other colors, like Alizarin Crimson, Viridian and the Thalo colors, are clearly transparent. Still other colors fall somewhere between: French Ultramarine, Payne's Gray, the Umbers and the Siennas.

The chart on page 77 illustrates the blending of colors. While only two contrasting colors are used for each panel, see how the blendings give the impression that more colors have been added.

In the first row Cadmium Yellow Medium is the top color. When it is blended with Cadmium Red Light, a color of the same weight in pigment, the two colors do very little mingling. In contrast, witness the mingling when the Cadmium Yellow is blended with the strong-staining Alizarin Crimson. The second row reveals the numerous shades of grays that result when warm and cool colors are blended. In the third row, note the interesting colors produced by blending black (until recently, taboo on the purist's palette) with single basic colors.

WATERCOLOR BRUSHES   In choosing brushes you can either pay the price necessary for good red sable brushes or acquire cheap brushes that are short-lived and never satisfactory. However, there is some compromising that can be done. Pictured below are four brushes:

First, the sable brush that will be used the most for general painting. Recommended sizes: nos. 4, 8 and 12. The following two flat, soft-haired brushes can be purchased in the less expensive ox-hair variety and will be found to be quite workable. A bristle stencil brush concludes the selection. This brush can be used for scrubbing out unwanted passages of color and is also useful for textural effects. A short-haired bristle oil painting brush can be used for the same purpose, but if you use one, restrict its use to watercolor.

Brushes courtesy M. Grumbacher, Inc.

M. GRUMBAC.

79

BRUSH TECHNIQUE

1 Hold the brush a distance away from the ferrule for general watercolor painting. This allows for greater ease and broader handling while working, particularly when applying color over a large area.

2 In contrast, the brush is held by the ferrule to maintain control when sharp accents or fine details are rendered.

3 As you work with the brush you will discover that much can be learned from the oriental school of brush handling. Holding the brush perpendicularly and grasping it just above the ferrule with the thumb and first two fingers will produce a finely delineated sharp stroke.

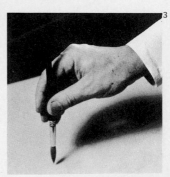

4 Also practice strokes by pulling the brush away from you and using your small finger when necessary for balance.

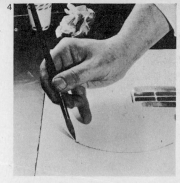

5 A series of ovals demonstrate how finely the strokes can be controlled by handling the brush in this manner.

6 A variation is shown here. The brush is still held in the upright position, but now the third and fourth fingers are employed. With such a firm grasp, the wrist and the arm can contribute in producing loose-appearing but actually well-controlled lines covering large areas.

7 The medium-wide, flat sable brush is useful in producing stylized strokes such as shown on page 84. Thin and thick

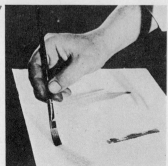

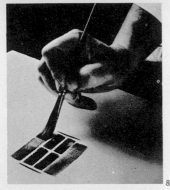

flowing lines can be produced by first using the edge or corner of the brush and then turning it on its flat side. A dry-brush effect can be produced by applying semi-moist color over a rough-surfaced paper, just grazing the paper with the brush.

8 Window panes and similar shapes that are the approximate width of the flat brush being used can be painted in a single stroke.

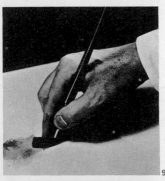

9 Interesting textures are achieved by placing the brush close to the paper and pressing its hairs. Broken color as well as texture, representing grass and foliage, can be accomplished in this manner.

10 This photograph shows how a broken or sketchy wash of color can be applied.

11 The wide, flat brush is becoming increasingly popular. It is excellent for wetting the paper preparatory to painting and for laying large washes of color. There is an aquarelle brush available that is one inch wide. It has a specially designed handle that comes to a pointed, chisel-like edge. This edge is useful in removing semi-moist color from areas in which you want the paper to show through (birch trees placed against a heavy green background, for example).

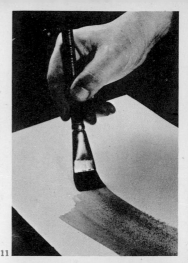

11

12 The wide flat brush can also produce thin lines if you use the corner edge.

If you take care of your brushes they will last a long time. Rinse thoroughly after use, and squeeze the hairs of a brush to remove the surplus water. At the same time, re-shape the brush and place it upward in a jar or holder reserved for storing brushes. A help in preserving your brushes is an occasional washing with mild soap and lukewarm water.

12

Here are a series of practice strokes which were produced with the previously described brushes. Exercises like these show you what can be accomplished by brushwork.

WASHES As you acquire facility in handling your brushes, you will find it much easier to control water-color washes.

In doing a *flat wash,* tilt your board forward at a slight angle to help keep the wash flowing. Dip your brush into the mixed color and apply it across the top of the paper. Then, gathering the color that has accumulated at the bottom of the stroke, repeat the motion, allowing a slight overlapping. Dip the brush into the color regularly to maintain an even flow.

The *graded wash* is applied with the board at the same angle. Again dip your brush into the mixed color and run it along the top of the paper. Follow with clear water, swiftly repeating the stroke and slightly overlapping the stroke of color. Repeat the motion, each time adding more water until the color blends into the white of the paper.

The *granulated wash* is useful in imparting interesting texture to an area. Select a couple of colors that

have an opaque or semi-transparent quality. (Try a mixture of Yellow Ochre and Cobalt Blue for this exercise.) With the board at the same slight angle, apply the mixture at the top of the paper, as in doing the flat wash, and cover the area. While the wash is still wet, tip the board back and forth. Some of the color will settle in the hollows of the paper and will dry with an interesting textural effect. This wash is most effective on a rough surface.

The painting of skies demands expert handling and control of color washes. It is only with constant practice that you achieve the sense of timing that tells you when to add color, how fluid it should be, and which color will predominate.

A very fluid wash results in a complete blending of colors but demands much control to keep the various colors from running together.

A fairly fluid wash enables you to achieve a more controlled blending and, consequently, more defined forms.

In a semi-moist wash you can add color that will not flow as freely or blend as easily as the washes above, but it results in better control.

THE LIMITED PALETTE   In the following sections some color combinations are suggested. Use them, but also make up several of your own. As with oil paints, experiment with a limited number of colors. The approach used on page 77 shows blending and super-imposing color washes. This will be of help in discovering new combinations for painting subjects of your own choosing.

The watercolor reproduced above is an example of a painting created with a limited palette. The original watercolor was not large—13 inches by 16 inches—and was done with four colors. Painted several years ago, it has always been one of my favorites and has been shown throughout the country in major exhibitions.

USING TWO COLORS The nature of a winter subject generally causes the beginning painter to think in terms of cool color, with possibly a bit of warm color for contrast. Here we use only two colors—Burnt Umber and Thalo Blue—to paint a typical winter scene. And, most important, the warm Burnt Umber is the key color in producing the vital grays.

Burnt Umber

Thalo Blue

WATERCOLOR DEMONSTRATION 1:
Using Two Colors

1 Make a pencil sketch on a quarter sheet of cold-pressed paper. Now paint the sky, using the Blue with a touch of Umber to warm and gray it. Paint the snow bank next, intensifying your color strength, and then do the large tree.

2 With the dark foreground

2

and the lighter sky area established, it will be easier to paint the distant hills in their correct value. Leave part of the paper white to depict the snow on the hilltop.

3 Finally, do the middle area and the trees. Paint the shadows of the trees on the snow as deftly as possible to utilize the whiteness of the paper.

3

Here are two more subjects painted with just two colors. At the top, Cadmium Orange and Cobalt Blue impart a late afternoon quality to the distant range of mountains.

Below, the character of a winter scene is captured by using only Payne's Gray and Yellow Ochre. Keep experimenting with only two colors; you will be surprised at what can be accomplished with so limited a palette!

Cobalt Blue

Cadmium Orange

Payne's Gray

Yellow Ochre

USING THREE COLORS A maximum amount of color can be obtained by using three colors—red, yellow and blue. However, a distinctive and more subtle color arrangement can be achieved.

In this demonstration I retain only the blue, a Cobalt, and add Raw Sienna and Hookers Green. The potential of this combination is seen on the following pages.

Raw Sienna

Hookers Green

Cobalt Blue

1

2

WATERCOLOR DEMONSTRATION 2: Using Three Colors

1 Make a pencil drawing of the subject, as shown on page 91.

2 Using clear water, proceed to moisten the cloud areas and, while the paper is still wet, quickly paint in the sky. If some of the blue should run into a cloud area, remove it with a dry brush or blotter. With practice you will be able to judge how moist the paper should be to control the running of the color. The rest of the color washes will be much easier to apply, as they are painted fairly flat, and you can allow an area to dry before painting the adjacent color. The foreground may be more of a problem: all three colors must be blended pleasingly to avoid a flat look. However, do not be too concerned if the colors run into each other. Often you can achieve

an exciting quality in your watercolor when this blending takes place.

3 At the conclusion of the previous stage we arrived at a fairly comprehensive color arrangement of what could be accomplished with three colors. From now to the finish we can concentrate upon intensifying those colors. First, paint the shaded areas, and immediately the subject will take on a more solid appearance. The modeling of the trees and their dark areas are achieved by mixing all three colors together. Whenever possible, try to mix the colors on the paper rather than on the palette: a more vibrant color will result. The painting of details should be left until the last. It is in this phase that we will give distinguishing textures to the subject. Place some sharp lines over the light and dark areas of the houses in the foreground to suggest the clapboards. Then give the foreground added emphasis by painting sharp accents in the grass and rock areas. The painting is now complete.

Colors straight from the tube that possess a grayed quality are useful in painting certain subdued subjects. A typical example is shown at the top of the page, using Chromium Oxide Green, Light Red and Payne's Gray to produce the rainy-day street scene. In contrast, bright colors—Cadmium Yellow Light, Alizarin Crimson and French Ultramarine—were used to execute the sunny subject.

USING FOUR COLORS The colors used for this demonstration have been selected to produce a scheme of harmonious grays. The Yellow Ochre is grayed primary yellow, the Light Red a primary red; and the French Ultramarine may be grayed by using Payne's Gray. You will find that these colors result in a low key. Thus it is best to choose subjects that lend themselves to such a mood. Here, I have selected a mining scene.

WATERCOLOR DEMONSTRATION 3:
A Low-Key Subject

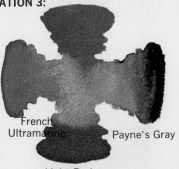

Yellow Ochre

French Ultramarine

Payne's Gray

Light Red

1 (P. 96) As the sky is the key to this subject, paint it first, moistening the entire area with clear water and, while still wet, quickly brushing a wash of Light Yellow Ochre over it. Before this dries, float the remaining three colors over the wash, leaving clear the area which halos the building. Follow this with light, flat washes of Payne's Gray, Light Red and Yellow Ochre in the foreground. Use French Ultramarine to portray the distant smoke, and add a touch of Yellow Ochre at the right of the smoke area.

2 (P. 96) Using the four colors at almost their full strength, now paint the foreground. Leave a little area of white where the green of the foliage meets the dark gray area. This is to depict a light edge that will remain in the finished picture.

3 (P. 97) Paint the distant mountains in a flat manner, taking care to retain the shape of the smoke. Next paint the large red building, using Light Red neutralized slightly with Payne's Gray.

95

1

Where the building rises toward the sky add more Payne's Gray to accent its dark, almost ominous shape.

4 In the final stage, model the mountains and darken them at their peaks. This will invest them with greater strength. Then paint the buildings against the smoke and mountain areas. Develop

2

3

the middleground contours and place foreground details in the railroad and path. Also add a few figures in the foreground, along with the telegraph poles, to lend scale to the subject. Complete the subject by giving texture to the cluster of foliage at the base of the picture and indicating tree trunks and some branches.

4

WATERCOLOR "QUICKIES"   Up to now our knowledge of watercolor has been acquired through disciplined exercises in handling the brush, washes and
limited color combinations. Because watercolor is a
medium in which technique is so important, it is
advisable to experiment occasionally.

One instructive approach is the making of quick
color impressions. These "quickies" are best practiced
in the studio, and the object is to obtain a fresh, free
style through a fast handling of the medium. They
should be done on a small scale; you can use the
reverse side of discarded watercolors.

The subject matter can be of your own choosing:
memory sketches of scenes you have previously
painted or observed, cloud formations, the moods of
a past season, places you have visited. At the start
you may want to sketch the subject with a few rough
lines, but as you progress, gradually eliminate all preparatory lines and paint directly with the brush. Most
important, do not spend more than five or ten minutes
on each sketch. You will undoubtedly make a batch
of sloppy quickies, but every so often one will turn
out with a fresh handling and a color effect that will
please you. And you will be even further pleased if you
take the time to mat those that have interesting possibilities. They may stimulate ideas for larger paintings.

Try painting quickies immediately after you have
had a walk through a country lane or city street. Sun-
sets and nocturnes are also rewarding subjects for
quick studio sketches. Finally, experiment with various
techniques when doing quickies. Do a series of
sketches in a wet manner, others in dry-brush, then
in a combination of techniques—but do them quickly!

Some typical quickies are shown above. They range in size from approximately 6 by 8 to 8 by 10 inches, and each was painted in from five to ten minutes.

A FULL COLOR PALETTE   We have seen what can be accomplished with a limited palette. A full color palette is used in this demonstration, but the subject still restricts the range of colors. A warm red dominates, and the absence of sky stresses this effect. The remaining colors are selected as foils for the red and serve to enhance it.

We will also utilize some technical devices in order to obtain textural effects. Watercolor painting lends itself well to such devices, but the student must be wary of overdoing them.

Along with employing a full color palette, I suggest that you use a full sheet of watercolor paper. It is good practice to vary the sizes of the paper on which you work. Too many students get used to working one size, generally on a one-quarter or one-half sheet. Then, when confronted with a full sheet of paper, they tighten up in their handling of color.

Just remember to mix more color than you think you will need, and use as large a brush as possible. Do just enough preliminary penciling to act as a guide for the placing of the color washes to follow. If the subject is a complicated one it is wise to make one or two small thumbnail sketches as a color guide for the large painting.

When you work to a small or medium size, the paper surface is less important than the quality. However, when you work full size, you will find it is easier to manipulate large color washes on a rough-textured paper. Also, make certain that the paper is of sufficient weight—200-lb. or 300-lb. is ideal. Or, you might consider using a watercolor or illustration board. This weight will prevent buckling.

WATERCOLOR DEMONSTRATION 4:
A Subdued Subject in Full Color

1 After penciling in the composition, apply a ground wash over the building, ash can and street. The wash is a combination of Alizarin Crimson and Cadmium Red Light with a slight touch of Yellow Ochre. Do not stir the mixture thoroughly; the colors will blend together on the paper. When dry, the area will possess very subtle passages of warm (Cadmium Red Light) and cool (Alizarin Crimson) tones.

2 Now apply paint to the shaded areas of the houses, the barrel in the foreground, and the shadows cast against the brick walls by the hanging wash, using the previous mixture of colors, and incorporating a generous amount of Light Red.

3 Apply a thin, flat preliminary wash of light yellow over the wooden annex, boxes, hydrant and fence. When this is dry, give the fence a wash of Raw Umber. Then paint the grass and bushes with Cadmium Yellow Light, floating Raw Umber and Thalo Green into the yellow.

4 Continue painting with flat color washes over the windows, door, figures and cement areas. Also render the delicate shadows of the hanging wash in a flat manner, using Cobalt Blue and Alizarin Crimson. Follow by painting the woodwork around the windows with Thalo Green.

5 Give the stone step area and wall a flat wash of Davy's Gray with an added touch of Payne's Gray, and allow it to dry. Then model the shaded areas with a deeper tone of the two grays, and into the wet mixture drop a bit of Burnt Sienna. While these areas are still damp, use a razor blade to impart a textural effect of crumbling old stone. (See photograph below.) Last, paint the shaded areas of the wooden annex, the doorway, the figures on the steps and street, and so on.

As described in step 5, a light wash of Davy's Gray has been laid over the stone area and permitted to dry. This is followed by a light application of Payne's Gray, into which a touch of Burnt Sienna has been dropped. Using the sharp edge of a razor blade at a slight angle, stroke the wet mixture in a semicircular manner. Some of the paint is removed through this method, revealing the original light gray undertone. Allow the surplus paint accumulated with the blade to dry, making no attempt to flatten it out. Use a small sable brush to add a few sharp dark accents.

6 It is always a problem to decide how much detail to render in a painting. As this painting is a close view of the subject, much more detail should be rendered than in the mining scene. The bricks in the building are important but cannot be painted with too precise a stroke. I used a sable flat brush, as shown in the accompanying photograph. Once you have painted the street, the subject is nearly completed.

6

The flat sable brush is most useful when a very precise or stylized stroke is wanted. Here is a typical example, employing the brush to render the bricks of the building.

7 Now paint in the final details—the clothesline, and the delicate branches of the tree—

using a fine-pointed sable brush. The same brush is also used for sharp accents. In areas where the color seems too harsh refine it by washing it down with the stiff bristle brush. The painting is completed after you have touched up accents in the washed down areas.

COLOR ROUGHS   In a previous section, I covered the making of rough pencil or charcoal compositions preparatory to painting a subject. These sketches go a step further. At first glance they resemble watercolor quickies. While they are accomplished in a short time, they are made to serve a different purpose: they will help you to determine a color arrangement that will best interpret the subject.

When you are working outdoors and have decided on the composition you want, make one of these preliminary "color notes," especially if you have any doubts about the planning of your color. Even where the color arrangement might seem quite resolved, a rough will be a good investment in keeping your color cleaner and less worked over, and the statement of your subject more fresh and direct.

A FULL COLOR COMPOSITION Here we have a subject colorful in itself that can employ the full range of colors, and painted on a bright day at a time of year when the color was at its height.

A full sheet of paper was again used for this demonstration. I referred to a small color sketch of the subject as I painted the large watercolor. My chief concern was establishing the correct color *values*. You must remember that in a small sketch just a dab of color to indicate an object can suffice. However, when you work large, that dab must have more substance; the drawing, values and color are equally important and must be correct. And what makes watercolor a difficult medium is that frequently these three elements must be managed all at the same time!

WATERCOLOR DEMONSTRATION 5:
A Bright Subject in Full Color

1 (See previous page.) First paint the water area with a mixture of Thalo Blue and Cobalt, using only a very faint tint of color toward the horizon and allowing the white paper to suggest the distant glare. Now add more of the color mixture, gradually intensifying the tone of the water as it approaches the bait house. Give the sky a wash of light Yellow Ochre, and, while it is still wet, float in some of the same color mixture used for the water. Next apply a wash of bright Yellow Ochre over the beach foreground, middleground and background areas and allow it to dry. Note how the pattern of the subject is clearly discernible although very little actual color appears. Then paint the areas surrounding the bait house. Keep in mind that the red color of the house will even-

2

tually be rendered as brilliantly as possible. Therefore the colors which surround it should be neutralized with a touch of Davy's Gray. This is true only of the shaded parts; the lights have to be kept clear and bright to reflect sunlight.

2 Paint the middle distance, using Yellow Ochre, Raw Umber, Burnt Sienna and Hookers Green Deep, with Cadmium Yellow Light to brighten the sunlit areas. As you paint the distant areas, add more blue to increase the look of recession.

3 Apply a wash of Cadmium Red Light mixed with a bit of Cadmium Orange over the light and dark sides of the red bait house. When this is dry, add Alizarin Crimson with a light touch of Cobalt Blue and Cadmium Red Light to the shadow areas. Then add more Cadmium Red at the lower part of the shadowed side to depict the glow that reflects the warm ground base. Finally paint the roof with a mixture of Ivory Black tinged with Thalo Green, and supply accents in the area surrounding the bait house.

3

THE FIGURE IN WATERCOLOR A figure rendered in watercolor has to be done much more deftly than a figure in oil painting. In the latter medium you can work on the figure, making whatever corrections are necessary and spending as much time as needed. It can be completely scraped out and repainted, if desired, without betraying any sign of struggle.

In a watercolor, on the other hand, a figure can be scrubbed out, but a certain amount of freshness is lost. I find it is most helpful to make separate drawings of any figures before placing them in a watercolor.

First try to capture the spirit of the pose or gesture. Then use a few lines to indicate the modeling of light and shade..

The sections of the water-colors reproduced here were made from preliminary drawings like those shown on pages 110–111. I feel that by using such an approach you can paint figures with more confidence.

A FIGURE COMPOSITION   In addition to being concerned with drawing, in a composition involving figures, it is most important to make the color arrangement as vital as possible. Strong, contrasting color schemes should be used, particularly in the area where you want the viewer's eye to linger. Elsewhere, in subordinate areas, the color can be modified.

It is worth your time to make a comprehensive pencil drawing of a figure composition. With this accomplished you are then free to concentrate on the arrangement of color. Make some preliminary color notes of the composition, in its entirety or in sections, to help you plan the best possible color scheme (p. 106). These notes can be extremely rough, with drawing a secondary consideration, as they are to act only as guides.

WATERCOLOR DEMONSTRATION 6:
A Subject with Figures

1 Make a pencil drawing to lay out the general composition of the subject, as on the preceding page.

2 Cover the entire paper with light washes of the various colors that will act as a guide for the more saturated color to follow. This stage can be likened to a "feeling out" process; no commitment has been made, and any color can still be changed if it will improve the overall arrangement. A figure composition is easier to control when approached in this manner. If strong color is used in any one area at the start, the rest of the composition must be painted to the key of that color.

3 Now you can start using color to its full intensity. Paint the figures in the foreground in full color. Before going on with the background, establish the dark of the two open windows. This will provide a standard for color values when painting the rest of the background area.

4 Paint the background. Then, subdue the color in

2

3

some areas, intensify it in others, and generally refine the color. Take care not to apply color in a heavy manner over a dry, previously painted area, for you may disturb the under-color. This is what causes muddy color or a woolly look to a water-color. Brush your overlaying color on with a light, flowing, deft stroke.

4

A WINTER SUBJECT IN WATERCOLOR What you have learned in painting a winter subject with oil color can be applied also to watercolor. Painting too blue a sky and raw violet snow shadows should be avoided. The big difference between the two mediums is in the application of white. With oil color the white areas are built up with a layer of paint; in watercolor the untouched white paper serves. And it is most important that these white areas of pure paper remain untouched, in order to attain a brilliance impossible to achieve with paint.

WATERCOLOR DEMONSTRATION 7: A Winter Subject

1 Make a pencil drawing of the subject, lightly indicating the principal objects in the composition.

2 This second stage (upper right) is vital in painting a snow scene. Using a diluted blue, paint a wash over the shaded areas of the subject. An immediate pattern of light and dark will be established, which will act as an important key throughout the rest of the painting. While the wash is applied

2

quickly, be careful to retain the original white paper for the light areas.

3 When the wash is dry, proceed with the painting, deftly, so as not to disturb the undercolor. Where you must paint over the wash, work with a full brush; where the wash harmonizes with the rest of the painting, allow it to remain untouched. Again, retain as much of the white paper as you can to show the glare of the snow.

3

BLOCKING OUT DEVICES   So far, our approach to the technique of watercolor has been in a direct manner. Now we arrive at some methods that probably sparked the expression, "Watercolor is a bag of tricks!" Here is one such trick, which will help you to retain areas of the original white surface of the paper. The importance of this you have already learned.

Let us assume that a white house is the focal point of your picture. The area of white could probably be kept by painting around it. It is when white areas are intricate in shape or small in size that they become difficult to hold.

Various methods can be employed to temporarily block out such portions. The most popular is the use of a liquid frisket. After you have carefully penciled the designated area, apply the frisket with a small, soft-haired brush. Since the liquid is gray in color, you are able to see which portion of the paper has been covered. It will dry in a short time, and you can then proceed to paint.

When the painting is dry, the frisket can be removed by rubbing your fingers gently over the coated area. You can then do whatever touching up is necessary.

A substitute for liquid frisket is rubber cement thinned out enough to make it flow easily. There is a tendency however, for some rubber cements to produce a stain. Whenever possible, use a razor or a sharp knife for minute details after the painting has dried. It is difficult to obtain a clean hair-line with the frisket. On the opposite page, the block at the upper left (1) illustrates how the white paper shows through a color wash after liquid frisket has been removed. There follows a demonstration of how frisket works.

2 First, a pencil drawing is made. **3** The liquid frisket is then applied with a small, pointed brush to the areas that are to remain white. **4** When the frisket is dry, the desired colors are painted over the blocked area, including the frisket itself. **5** When the paint is dry, the frisket is rubbed off gently with the fingertips. **6** Then color is applied over the remaining areas.

The paper frisket placed on the paper.

MASKING TAPE AS A FRISKET Paper masking tape can also be used as a blocking-out device if the area to be retained is of a simple shape. The plates on this page illustrate typical items that are easy to make from masking tape. They can be cut with a pair of scissors or a razor and then pressed on the paper. It may be necessary to piece together sections of the tape to obtain larger or more intricate shapes. The painting procedure is the same as with the liquid frisket.

The paper painted and frisket removed.

SEVERAL TECHNICAL DEVICES In this demonstration a subject has been chosen that lends itself to the use of technical devices throughout its development. However, the beginner should be wary of overdoing the use of such devices. There is always the danger of concentrating unduly on the technical aspect of a subject. Remember that design and color are far more important considerations. Here, I have deliberately emphasized technical devices for the purpose of instruction.

WATERCOLOR DEMONSTRATION 8: Special Techniques

1 Render the usual pencil drawing, giving a general idea of the composition of the subject.

2 Before any color is applied, cover areas that are to remain white with a liquid frisket: For example, some of the branches and leaves of the tree, along with a few sharp lines. (It may be hard

2

to discern the frisket in the illustration above, since it reproduces in the same color as the penciling.) After the frisket has dried, begin the painting by giving the sky area a wash of clear water. Then, while the paper is still wet, brush in the appropriate sky colors. Follow this by giving the sunlit areas a preliminary wash of their approximate coloring. Then paint the windows, which should be done at this point because the color around them is to be painted much darker.

3 Next commence to paint the houses in the background. This will establish the glaring effect of the win-dows. Use Alizarin Crimson and Cobalt Blue as the prin-cipal colors. Apply only a wash of the blue over the shaded area in the most dis-tant building. Then paint some sharply placed darks over the background to give it more luminosity. Place dark color behind the laun-dry, also, but first paint the clothesline.

4 Now paint the shaded areas and the shadows cast by the houses, adding Yellow Ochre, Light Red and Davy's Gray to your palette. A touch of Cadmium Red Light will help to produce a warm glow in the building behind the still unpainted wall. Put some color details in that. When

the entire painted surface is dry, remove the frisket, exposing the white paper underneath.

5 Place a wash of Davy's Gray over the wall area, and while it is wet, add touches of Payne's Gray and Burnt

5

Sienna. Just before the paint is dry, pull a razor blade over some of the areas, producing a texture of rough stone (see photograph, upper left). Now depict the wooden door and cast shadow in the foreground. While this area is still wet, paint in tufts of grass and broken textures of earth. Stop to check the overall effect. If any passages seem too dark, dip a stencil brush or a stiff bristle brush in clean water and rub it over the area (see photograph, lower left). Remove enough color so that the corrected passage harmonizes with the surrounding area. The same brush can be used for other textural effects—faded color, broken surfaces.

6

6 Now render the wall in the foreground, using a flat sable brush to produce the brick areas. Select a brush which will enable you to paint the bricks with a single stroke, as shown in the photograph at the right. Vary the color of the bricks with a touch of blue. Paint the bush to the left of the wall with Hookers Green and a touch of Burnt Sienna. Leave a halo around the edges of the bush to indicate the glaring light striking it. Then paint the truck, letting Thalo Blue dominate. Follow by painting the tree, again leaving a white edge of sunlight. Finally, use the razor blade to pick out white highlights, as in the bottom photograph.

USING THE WHITE OF PAPER   It has been stated that one of the chief charms of a watercolor is the effect created by areas of untouched white paper. While the medium has not yet reached the stage of the avant-garde "white on white," there is no doubt of white's enhancing quality.

An interesting exercise is to select a subject that will allow the white paper to occupy the major area of the composition, such as the one chosen for this demonstration. The objective is not to make the white area too obvious but to blend it in value with the rest of the colored areas.

It might be helpful for you to first make a separate, fast, black-and-white sketch, using either pencil or charcoal. In this preliminary planning you can decide on the strongest possible arrangement before proceeding to use color.

WATERCOLOR

DEMONSTRATION 9:

Using Paper's White

1   Do a pencil drawing to establish the composition. At this stage you should have an idea of how much untouched white paper you want to retain.

2 After determining that a large area of the house is to be left white, paint part of the background. Follow this by painting in the shadows. These shadows are important, for they serve two purposes: They accent the whiteness of the house; and they add interest to what could be a monotonous area. Note how the cast shadow in the left corner keeps the eye from wandering out of the composition.

3 Now paint the tree, completing the background. Next do the windows, whose dark areas also spark the surrounding white paper. And the white paper in turn enhances the color of the flowers in the upper window. If at any point you wish to lighten an area already painted, and providing you are working on rough paper, use a hard eraser or a piece of fine sandpaper. This method will often give life to an area dulled by too many washes of color. Place a few sharp accents on the house, sidewalk and street to complete the painting.

THE VIGNETTE   To continue our exploration of white paper as part of a design, we now come to the vignette, whose primary use is in interpreting a subject decoratively. The vignetted *shape,* a series of lost-and-found edges, is its chief attraction. It looks simple to achieve, but this appearance is very deceiving, for the vignette must be carefully designed.

One approach to creating a vignette is to use a completed watercolor as a guide. Initially, work to a small size (an eight-by-ten-inch trimmed paper). Lightly pencil an enveloping shape, pleasingly abstract in itself, leaving at least a two-inch margin. Then sketch in the main lines of the subject. (See the pencil drawing below.) Start to paint from the center of interest, simplifying the color areas as you go along. As you approach the penciled outline, moisten the edges first

with clear water to soften the subsequent color. In your next attempt, reverse this procedure by first painting the soft edges and then adding stronger color as you work toward the center.

INK BASES Watercolor combines very well with other mediums; and particularly with ink. Formerly, artists employed watercolor as an embellishment to an inked drawing. The result was not a painting but a colored drawing. This technique was especially popular for architectural subjects, as it enlivened the drab black and white rendering.

I have been experimenting during the past few years with this combination when doing street scenes. However, I attempt to use ink as a textural aid. Reproduced above in black and white are two renderings of the same subject. At the left is a colored pen and ink drawing; at the right, what I am attempting to achieve ideally. Here, every effort is made to avoid the mechanical line of pen and ink. The paper is moistened to help destroy hard lines, and spattering is used, rather than crosshatching, for halftone and texture. Sometimes watercolor is applied while the inked base is still wet; at other times, when the ink is thoroughly dry.

At present I find this technique more workable in the studio than on the spot.

WATERCOLOR DEMONSTRATION 10: Using an Ink Base

1 Shown here is the first stage of a watercolor with an ink base. It is necessary for the bulk of the work to be done on a wet or semi-moist surface. Since it is impossible to keep the entire surface constantly wet, moisten a small section at a time. Along with the pen line, you can use spattering or pouncing with a sponge for textures. Waterproof sepia and diluted black inks are used at this stage. Thus it is easy to re-moisten any areas without disturbing the original ink.

2 Watercolor is applied over the various areas. While several washes of transparent watercolor can be brushed over the inked surface, you must be careful when you use semi-opaque colors. They will tend to obliterate the ink base. This technique allows me to obtain textural qualities impossible with regular watercolor.

WATERCOLOR DEMONSTRATION 11:

Using a Black Ink Base

1 In this demonstration, use a black ink as a base. Work with a fine pen to do the drawing, being careful not to make too firm or solid a line. Part of the paper can be moistened as you work to help produce an occasional blurred line. Dilute your ink to a wash to suggest halftone and shaded areas.

First paint the center building, using principally Indian Red, Naples Yellow, Thalo Blue and Raw Umber. Then paint the corner store, adding a Yellow Ochre to the blue to produce a green. For the sky area use Cobalt Blue with a touch of Thalo Green;

and for the street, a light wash of Indian Red.

2 Now paint the houses which flank the center one, using a base of Davy's Gray for the lower part of the house at the left. As a base for the upper portion, use diluted Thalo Blue, applying a bit of Yellow Ochre while the blue is still wet. For the corner house, use Yellow Ochre and Raw Umber as a base.

3 In the final stage, render the texture of clapboards on the wooden houses, which will immediately strengthen

2

their appearance. Then paint the background. Finally, put in the details. In checking the various colors used you will discover how semi-opaque color can obliterate or tone down the ink base. This is true of Indian Red used in the shaded areas of the center building.

An ink undertone, used in this manner, is like an underpainting for oil. It carries the drawing, defines form, and influences the final color and tonal relationships.

3

PAINTING FROM A PENCIL SKETCH   Frequently you will find it is not feasible to make a painting directly on the spot. You can content yourself by just sketching the subject, but if you wish to do a studio painting at a later date, you might consider the following method.

Assume that you are at work, sketching any subject available. Suddenly, possibly due to a changing light, you spot a subject that possesses an exciting arrangement of color. Quickly sketch it, roughing in the shaded areas as you go along. At the same time—particularly if the color effect is fleeting—make pencil notations of the varied colors directly on the sketch. A typical sketch with such notations is shown below.

A variation of this method is to use marginal notes with arrows pointing to the various colors of the subject. Such a sketch is shown on page 136.

The pencil-notated drawing on the facing page served as a reference for the watercolor reproduced above. One of the important objectives in developing such a painting in the studio is to try to impart the illusion that the subject was painted on the spot. It should not look labored, as do so many outdoor subjects when they are painted indoors. One way to help overcome this overworked look is to paint wet-into-wet—that is, to work as much as possible with the color brushed into a wet surface. The occasional flowing of one color into an adjacent one helps to impart a free "outdoors" look to the subject.

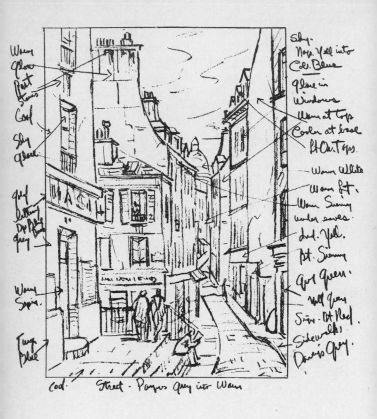

Here is a pencil sketch with marginal notes indicating color. It is good practice to paint the subject in the studio as soon as possible, while the visual impression of the scene is still quite fresh. This impression, when supplemented with your notes, will give you a better chance of turning out a successful painting.

PAINTING OVER NOTES Using a pad of good quality paper, receptive to watercolor and a pencil of medium grade, follow the same procedure described on page 134. This time, however, you will paint directly over your sketch. Pencil the color notations *lightly*, and shade where necessary.

WATERCOLOR DEMONSTRATION 12: Painting over Notes

1 The sketch shown on page 137 was done on good quality paper. The colors and tonal notations were penciled in on the spot. As you work

with this method you will find yourself developing a shorthand to indicate colors.

2 Since you know in

3

advance just what colors you are going to use, you can almost completely develop each area to its full color as you go along. Here we have started with the area that backs the center of interest.

3 As the painting progresses, you can remove the penciled notations by erasing them lightly, taking care not to blemish the surface. Paint the figures and vegetable market, which is the center

4

of interest, and then paint the sky area. Lay a cool wash over the street in the fore-ground. Blend into a warmer tone as the wash recedes.

4 Paint the background, employing a cast shadow to help subdue any bright color that may detract from the center of interest. After you have put sharp details in the foreground, the background will recede still further.

CASEIN

Casein is a highly versatile medium increasing in popularity. It can be handled like watercolor, and when greatly diluted, it resembles watercolor. When used with just enough water to make it workable, it is opaque and becomes a gouache. Unlike the usual gouache, when varnished it resembles an oil painting. Or it can be used for the underpainting of a subject in oil color.

MATERIAL AND EQUIPMENT   Casein is available in tubes and comes in a wide range of colors. I suggest that you start with the same selection as those listed for watercolor painting. Later you may want to add some of the new brilliant colors now available, such as Thalo Yellow and Green and Grumbacher Red. You can use your watercolor brushes when working in a fluid manner or oil brushes (preferably new and used only for casein) for applying the paint heavily.

Casein is very fast-drying so a non-absorbent palette which retards drying should be used. Metal or plastic is best, but even a white dinner plate can be used. Generally, you need only water as a medium, but there is a drying-retarder available known as Casein Painting Medium.

Casein can be applied to almost any surface. Watercolor paper or a good grade of illustration board is excellent. Gesso board is good; it is a specially prepared absorbent canvas.

There is a varnish made for finishing a casein painting, and there is also a preparation known as Tuffilm, with which you can spray a protective glossy coating.

An example of how a power-
ful color (Thalo Green) can
be washed down to a delicate
tint is shown at the upper
left. Casein applied in an
opaque manner and then
transparently is illustrated in
the two following panels. The
black square with the over-
painted yellow strokes shows
the strong covering power of
casein. This is followed by the
same area of sky painted
first in an opaque and then in

a transparent manner.

At the left of the third row,
a painting knife has been
used to blend the casein
color, and in the next panel
the colors have been blended
by pouncing them with a stiff
brush. The reddish square
reveals how the color retains
its intensity even when it
is diluted; the black square
shows casein blended by a
technique employed in oil
painting.

142

CASEIN USED AS A GOUACHE   In our first demonstration, the casein paint will be applied in a gouache, or opaque, technique. Both watercolor and oil brushes can be used, the latter doing the bulk of the work. An illustration on watercolor board will serve best and should be done at a minimum size of 11-by-14 inches.

You can do a good deal more penciling of the subject when working with casein than you can with watercolor, which is transparent. Note the strong covering power of casein; light colors can be applied over dark colors without disturbing them. You can employ much of the brush handling that you learned while working in watercolor and oil, particularly the latter. When the painting is completed, it will have a matte finish. Frame it with glass, like a regular gouache painting. Or varnish it and place it in a heavy oil frame; visually it will be accepted as an oil painting!

CASEIN DEMONSTRATION 1:
Gouache Technique

1 (See previous page.) Pencil in the subject and indicate the light and shade areas. Using the casein opaquely—that is, with just enough water to make it workable—spot in the various colors. This approach is similar to working with oil color in a direct manner.

2 Apply the color freely, making no attempt to fill in any area solidly. Instead, allow the white background to show through so that your painting does not become tight too soon. You can always tighten it up at the final stage.

3 Now start painting in a more solid manner. At this stage, you should nearly complete the sky, background and houses. Model the tree in the foreground, establishing a degree of finish that will in turn establish the finish in the rest of the painting.

4 It is up to you to decide how detailed a finish you want. I prefer a painting kept

2

3

fairly free, as the subject looked at stage 2. However, I have purposely carried the subject further along to demonstrate the degree of finish that can be obtained.

4

Casein used as a watercolor (above); and as a gouache (below).

CASEIN ON A DARK-TONED SURFACE The strong covering power of casein paint is best revealed when you work on a dark-toned surface. By painting with the color diluted to a thin consistency you can allow the toned suface of the paper to affect the overlaying color. Where you want to obliterate the toned paper, apply the casein heavily.

In this demonstration, black paper is used. The paper has been mounted on stiff cardboard to prevent buckling. Also, a rigid surface will be more receptive to a final coating of varnish, if desired.

Other than roughly sketching the principal lines, you cannot do much preliminary penciling on the black background. Once this is done, the subject can be drawn with any light-colored casein paint.

CASEIN

DEMONSTRATION 2:

Using a Dark-toned Surface

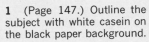

1 (Page 147.) Outline the subject with white casein on the black paper background.

2 Begin painting in the foreground area. The thinner the casein is applied the more it is affected by the black paper underneath. You will find that you can achieve bold effects that cannot be obtained when working on a regular white surface. (This and the next two steps are reproduced in black and white.)

3 A sunny effect is desired in the middle area, so apply the casein heavily, using just enough water to make the paint workable, and completely obliterate the black paper.

4 Now paint the background, thinning the casein in the shaded areas and brushing it on more heavily in the light. Paint the sky with solid color, similar to the sunny middle area, in order to achieve a luminous effect.

5 The completed subject is presented below in color. An area that shows the advantage of using a black surface can be seen in the red barn on the left. The red was painted fairly heavily at the base, but more water was used to thin the color as it neared the edge of the roof. Note that the thinned paint allowed the black paper to show through enough to darken the color tone. The color in the shaded areas of the foreground rocks was achieved in the same manner. Incidentally, the texture of the green foliage at the right was obtained by pouncing the wet color.

5

CASEIN VIGNETTES   Earlier I discussed the painting of vignettes in a transparent style. With casein you can paint either transparently or opaquely. At the same time you can take advantage of a toned surface. The subject shown here was painted on DeWint paper, which has an excellent working surface grayish-tan in color. It is most sympathetic to casein, particularly when the paper tone is allowed to show through.

CASEIN DEMONSTRATION 3: A Vignette

1   Pencil in the subject, and roughly outline the vignette. Apply the color from the outer edges inward. First wet the paper where the color is to dry with a soft edge.

transparent quality of the casein. Where you do not wish this effect apply the casein heavily. The white light on the house is painted in this manner.

2   The grayish-tan of the paper will enhance the

3   Leave the original paper to serve as the natural color

2

of the road and some of the rooftops. When you have finished, you will find that a vignette on toned paper produces a charming, decorative interpretation.

3

CASEIN ON GESSO BOARD   The brilliant white base of a gesso board or panel imparts a striking luminosity to casein colors. At the same time, interesting textures can be achieved by scraping the surface with various sharp instruments or with sandpaper.

You can make your own gesso panels by covering the smooth side of a masonite board with several coats of liquid gesso. But this is a time consuming task, and I advise you to purchase an already prepared panel.

Make your sketch as usual, using charcoal and then dusting off the surplus. The faint image can be reconstructed with any color you choose; blue is always satisfactory. Apply the paint thinly at first, gradually building up the colors. Where you want a particularly luminous effect, use a series of thin washes rather than a single application of heavy paint. Experiment with scraping areas to obtain unique textural effects. All such scraping should be done *before* the painting is varnished and becomes too hard to penetrate. Varnishing lowers the over-all tone; darks especially become much richer and have a glowing quality.

Some artists object to the shine of a varnished surface but still want the deep, rich tones that the varnish brings. The shine can be lessened by rubbing some picture wax over the surface once the varnish is completely dry. The wax will immediately cloud the color, but this cloudiness will disappear as the surface is rubbed in a circular motion with a soft rag. A slight sheen will appear that can be heightened to the degree desired by continual rubbing. If you do not wish to varnish the painting, the panel must be handled with extreme care, for the surface will scratch easily.

VARNISH OVER CASEIN   The right half of the painting below has been given a coating of casein varnish. Note how it lowers the tone and darks become richer. If varnished in its entirety, the painting would now resemble an oil and could be framed accordingly. It may be necessary to give a casein painting more than one coat of varnish to produce an even shine. Avoid applying varnish on damp days. Dampness in your brush may later produce a milky film over some areas of the painting. Another warning: Do not apply varnish immediately to a painting that has been stored in a cold room. Both varnish and painting should be at about the same temperature. Apply the varnish thinly.

OIL GLAZES OVER CASEIN   The reproduction above shows the lay-in of the subject accomplished with casein on canvas. The general color arrangement has been painted in a lighter key to allow for a lowering of the tone with the subsequent application of oil glazes. Remember to apply the color thinly whenever using casein for underpainting, particularly when working on a stretched canvas. An underpainting like this will give you a comprehensive idea of the final effect. You can even include such details as lettering.

After the casein painting has dried, it is given a coat of casein varnish. The varnish serves to isolate the casein and prevents the oil color, which is to follow,

from seeping into the casein base. When the varnish is dry to the touch you can proceed with the oil glazing or, where desired, apply the oil paint in a heavier manner for textural effects. You can use your copal painting medium to cut the oil paint to the consistency needed for glazing. The reproduction above shows the subject after receiving a series of warm, toned glazes.

It is important to remember that only oil paints are to be used once the varnish has been applied. To use casein over varnish or over oil paint would be to risk the possibility of having the casein flake off, since the varnished surface is no longer absorbent and cannot bind the casein.

A single painting is spread across these two pages. The left half illustrates how the subject looks with a pale, gray casein underpainting; and the right half, how it looks after oil color has been applied. The underpainting developed the subject in its approximate colors at the start, but here the approach differed, because only a

pale, restricted palette was
employed. Therefore many
more glazes were required to
attain a full color effect. But
the extra work produced a
warm, luminous quality impossible with straight oil
painting. You can apply the
oil heavily on some areas for
impasto effects. Or you can
glaze the areas to harmonize
with the rest of the painting.

157

GLOSSARY

ACCENT A sharp detail; to place a detail in a painted area for emphasis.

AQUARELLE 1. A method of painting watercolors without the use of white and employing only thin, transparent washes of color.
2. A painting done in this technique.
3. A brush, like Grumbacher 6142 or 6143, with flat, square face and side contour of a pointed brush. Handle is bevelled for scraping, burnishing, etc.

CAST SHADOW The dark area that results when a source of light has been intercepted.

COBALT DRIER Used with oil colors to accelerate drying time.

COMPLEMENTARY COLORS Colors opposite each other on a color wheel. (See Primary Colors and Secondary Colors.)

COPAL PAINTING MEDIUM A prepared medium made from copal resin and oil. Used for glazing with oil colors.

COROT CRAYONS Artists' chalk (semihard) made in a limited color range: Sanguine, Sepia, Black and White.

CROSS HATCHING A shading of the subject by drawing two sets of parallel lines which intersect, as in a grid.

DRY-BRUSH A technique in which paint or ink is applied sparingly with a semidry brush.

FERRULE The metal portion of the brush holding the hairs.

FIXATIVE A colorless fluid sprayed on pencil, charcoal drawings and pastel paintings to minimize dusting and smudging and to protect them from dirt.

FRISKET A device, usually of gummed paper, placed on the working surface to block out subsequent painting. When the paper is removed, the original surface is intact. Also available in liquid.

GESSO	A mixture of glue and whiting used as a ground for painting. Also made in a less absorbent prepared polymer base.
GOUACHE	1. Watercolor painting technique using white and opaque colors. 2. A general name for opaque watercolors (poster color, showcard color, designer's color, casein, etc.).
IMPASTO	The application of colors in a heavy manner, generally with a knife, causing the paint to stand out in relief.
IMPRIMATURA	A transparent tone that is applied to the canvas or paper before the general painting commences.
KEY	The general tone of a painting. When the subject is painted in dark tones it is referred to as a "low key"; when in light tones, as a "high key."
LAY-IN	The initial visualization of the subject on canvas, usually in a single color, preparatory to actual painting.
MAT	A heavy paper (mat board) frame which provides a border around a painting.
MATTE	A dull surface quality.
MEDIUM	1. A substance added to artists' colors to produce specific results: gloss, matte, texture; or to modify brushing characteristics, drying time, etc. 2. A designation of the type of color employed in a painting, for example: oil, watercolor, casein, Hyplar, pastel, etc.
MONOCHROMATIC	Consisting of one color in all its values.
PALETTE KNIFE	The knife used to remove surplus paint from the palette or to mix colors on the palette.
PAINTING KNIFE	A knife which differs from the above in having a more flexible blade and in being used for actual painting.
POUNCING	Applying color in a tapping motion, usually with a sponge, cloth or stencil brush.

PRIMARY COLORS	Red, Yellow and Blue. These colors are complementary to the Secondary Colors.
RETOUCH VARNISH	A varnish applied by spraying. 1. Used to bring out dull or "sunken-in" areas of color when painting is resumed after an interruption of work. 2. Used as a temporary protective varnish during period when painting is drying before application of a final varnish.
RIGGER BRUSH	A square-edged brush in a round ferrule.
SECONDARY COLORS	Green, Violet and Orange. These colors are complementary to the Primary Colors.
SCUMBLING	A general term to describe paint manipulation with a brush to achieve textural effects.
SKETCH	A rough or brief visualization of a subject or idea.
SPATTERING	Applying ink or color in flecks or drops by shaking from the end of a pen or brush, or by drawing a brush over a screen.
STAND OIL	A heavy-bodied, syrupy form of partially polymerized linseed oil which has the property of leveling brush strokes to produce a smooth, enamel-like surface.
STUDY	A comprehensive drawing or painting of a subject. Also a detail that can be used for reference in doing a finished painting.
UNDERPAINTING	A broad rendition of color and/or texture which is subsequently developed and finished in form, detail and color by overpainting and glazing.
VALUE	The relative lightness or darkness of colors or of gray.
VIGNETTE	A painting which is shaded off around the edges to make a pleasing shape, leaving a border of white or some other background color.
WASH	1. A highly fluid application of color. 2. A painting or a drawing done in this technique.

C